Blues Harmonica Level 2
The Tongue Blocking Method
by David Barrett

Online Audio

www.melbay.com/21054BCDEB

D1384907

Audio Contents

1 Table of Contents, Material Needed & About the Author	25 Five-Hole Octave Example Song
2 What Notes Can Be Bent	26 Five-Hole Octave Play-Along
3 Bending Exercises	27 Side Pull
4 Two-Note Combinations	28 Octave Pull-Slap
5 Bending Example Song	29 Octave Pull-Slap Example Song
6 Bending Example Song Play-Along	30 Single Note Pull-Slaps
7 Quartertone Bending	31 "Serious Fun" Chorus One Breakdown
8 Bending Example Song	32 "Serious Fun" Chorus Two Breakdown
9 Bending Example Song Play-Along	33 "Serious Fun" Chorus Three Breakdown
10 More Bending Exercises	34 "Serious Fun" Chorus Four Breakdown
11 More Bending Exercises	35 "Serious Fun" Chorus Five Breakdown
12 "Feelin' Good" Chorus One Breakdown	36 "Serious Fun" Chorus Six Breakdown
13 "Feelin' Good" Chorus Two Breakdown	37 "Serious Fun" Chorus Seven Breakdown
14 "Feelin' Good" Chorus Three Breakdown	38 "Serious Fun" Example Song
15 "Feelin' Good" Chorus Four Breakdown	39 "Serious Fun" Play-Along
16 "Feelin' Good" Chorus Five Breakdown	40 "Lick Train" Chorus One Breakdown
17 "Feelin' Good" Chorus Six Breakdown	41 "Lick Train" Chorus Two Breakdown
18 "Feelin' Good" Chorus Seven Breakdown	42 "Lick Train" Chorus Three Breakdown
19 "Feelin' Good" Chorus Eight Breakdown	43 "Lick Train" Chorus Four Breakdown
20 "Feelin' Good" Chorus Nine Breakdown	44 "Lick Train" Chorus Five Breakdown
21 "Feelin' Good" Chorus Ten Breakdown	45 "Lick Train" Chorus Six Breakdown
22 "Feelin' Good" Example Song	46 "Lick Train" Chorus Seven Breakdown
23 "Feelin' Good" Play-Along Track	47 "Lick Train" Example Example Song
24 Five-Hole Octaves	48 "Lick Train" Play-Along

Thanks to Diane Smith, Guri Stark, Dan Reyes and Dennis Carelli for proofreading

1 2 3 4 5 6 7 8 9 0

Visit us on the Web at www.melbay.com — E-mail us at email@melbay.com

Table of Contents

Material Needed

Harmonica   You will need a C and A major ten-hole diatonic harmonica for this book and recording.

Audio Player   Whether you are studying this course by yourself or with a harmonica instructor, the audio included with this book will be very helpful to make sure your notes are correct and your rhythm is strong. For easy audio navigation, the example numbers in black boxes are also the track numbers on your audio.

Continuing the Tongue Block Method

Book one in this series gave you the foundation of how to play single notes on the harmonica with good rhythm within the context of the 12 Bar Blues Progression. You also learned the three most common techniques used in tongue blocking: Slaps, Pulls and Octaves.

In the first half of this book we'll learn the second most important technique for blues harmonica playing—bending. Bending makes available to us notes that are not part of the natural tuning of the harmonica and gives us the ability to slide between notes for a bluesy effect.

The second half of the book is dedicated to playing great blues harmonica instrumentals that utilize all of the techniques we've studied.

About the Author

David Barrett is the world's most published author of blues harmonica instruction material. Having played saxophone and trumpet for many years, David already had a solid musical platform when he started to play the harmonica at age fourteen. By age sixteen he was already playing blues jam sessions and harmonica shows in the California Bay Area. By age eighteen he was studying music theory in college and started teaching harmonica at local music institutes. By age twenty he released his first book Building Harmonica Technique with Mel Bay Publications. David now runs the Harmonica Masterclass® Company full time, bringing lesson books, CDs, videos, private instruction, and workshops to players all around the world. Along with writing for multiple Ezines, David also writes monthly columns for magazines such as Blues Revue. David is the owner of School of the Blues in San Jose California where he accepts fly-in lessons on a regular basis. Visit www.harmonicamasterclass.com for information on blues harmonica workshops and for private lessons visit www.schooloftheblues.com.

David has worked and played with Charlie Musselwhite, Mark Hummel, Lee Oskar, Rod Piazza, James Harman, James Cotton, Gary Smith, Andy Just, Mark Ford, Billy Boy Arnold, Rick Estrin, Paul deLay, Jerry Portnoy, Gary Primich, Howard Levy, Magic Dick, Tom Ball, Sonny Jr., Annie Raines, Paul Oscher, Phil Wiggins, Brendan Power, Sam Myers, Snooky Pryor, Rob Paparozzi, Dennis Gruenling, Carlos del Junco, Mitch Kashmar, Joe Filisko, Jr. Watson, Steve Freund, John Garcia, and many more. He fronts his own band featuring John Garcia on guitar and vocals.

About the School of the Blues Lesson Series

School of the Blues is a school dedicated to the study of blues and all the styles it influenced. Founded in 2002 by educator David Barrett, the school thrives today as the center of blues education in the San Jose/San Francisco California Bay Area.

The instructors at the school and in this lesson series have on average twenty years teaching and performing experience. All of the instructors were hand picked to teach at the school for their playing skills, knowledge of their instrument and ability to teach all skill levels of private and group instruction. We are all dedicated to our craft and receive huge pleasure playing an active role in our students' musical and personal development as well rounded musicians.

This series is a continuation of this love for the music and its education. David Barrett is the administrator and coauthor of all the books. Many meetings took place with all of the instructors present to shape the outline of the books and to make sure that the experience and knowledge of the instructors was contained within each book.

A cornerstone to the School of the Blues instruction approach is showing a student how to apply what they learn. Purchasing Blues Harmonica Play-Along Tracks (MB21055M) is highly recommended to provide you with extended Play-Along Tracks to practice with. This series is also designed for students of other instruments to play together. If you have friends that play guitar, keyboard, bass or drums, tell them about this series so that you can grow together. There's nothing more fun than making music with other people.

We all wish you the best of luck in your studies. For more information about this series or to contact us, please visit www.schooloftheblues.com.

Chapter 1 – Bending

Bending is achieved by tuning your mouth to the pitch you desire to bend to. Lowering the pitch of your mouth is achieved by two movements of your tongue: 1) Your tongue must hump up to constrict the air passage. 2) Your tongue must move back to lower the resonant pitch of your mouth and thus lower the pitch of the reed you intend to bend.

Start by saying the vowel "E" in a draw tongue block anywhere on the lower six holes. "E" places the middle/back of your tongue under your upper set of teeth. This sets up the passage where the air will travel. You can feel the air only traveling between the roof of your mouth, the inner-sides of your teeth, and the top of your tongue. The center of the tongue then pushes up (like the "K" in "Key") to squeeze the air stream for the constriction needed (of which not a lot is needed). Your tongue then pulls back to bring the pitch of that reed down. Depending where you hump up your tongue, you might have very little movement back for the bend (such as a 6 draw), or you might have a large amount of movement to create the bend (such as the 3, 2 and 1 draw).

Each reed is a different length and different sounding pitch. The longer the reed, the lower the pitch and the slower its vibration. The shorter the reed, the higher its pitch and the faster its vibration. In the bending process, as you move your tongue back for the bend, it's frequency pulling the reed. In other words, as your tongue moves back, the resonant pitch of your mouth lowers and so does the pitch of the reed you're playing. This is best felt by whistling. Try to whistle a high note, then slowly slide the pitch down to the lowest note you can achieve. Notice that the wings of your tongue are touching your upper set of teeth and to lower the pitch you move your tongue back, and to raise the pitch your tongue moves forward. The process is the same for bending a note on the harmonica.

For the 6 draw, the front-middle of your tongue will move up, and not very much back. For the 4 draw, you'll move further up and back. You'll probably find the 4 draw to be one of your easier notes to bend. Reference the diagram at right to get a visual idea of where the tongue will be in relation to the roof of the mouth. Note that the tip of your tongue will be on the face of the harmonica for the tongue block.

When trying the 3 or 2 draw bend, most players don't move their tongue up high enough and far enough back. The 3 draw bend is achieved by having your tongue humped up somewhere near your back molars, resting on the gums. The 2 draw is further back, most of the time not touching the teeth at all, just the gums. The 1 draw is back and down a bit.

When performing the lower bends you might find it useful to drop your jaw. This lowers the resonant pitch of your mouth and should make tuning your mouth to the bend you desire to play easier.

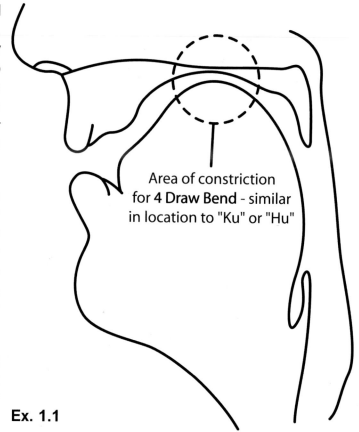

Area of constriction for **4 Draw Bend** - similar in location to "Ku" or "Hu"

Ex. 1.1

Another helpful hint for the lower draw bends is to think of raising the root of your tongue for the deeper bends. Since the front of your tongue is stuck on the face of the harmonica, the lowered pitch is achieved by humping up different parts of the tongue, across the length of the tongue. It will be hard to move the middle of the tongue far back enough to achieve the pitch needed for the lower bends. By humping the stem of the tongue up, you're able to access a part of the tongue that's already located very far back in the mouth. The main point is to experiment! Read this information over and over—you won't get it the first read through. Get to know what your tongue is doing in your mouth and where it's located relative to different places within the mouth.

What Notes Can Be Bent

Not every hole (note) on the harmonica can be bent, and not every hole that you can bend allows the same degree of bend. The amount of bend you can achieve is dictated by the distance (interval) between your draw and blow reed. Diagramed below is the chromatic scale. The chromatic scale lists every note available in our diatonic music system.

Ex. 1.2 A B♭ B C D♭ D E♭ E F G♭ G A♭ A

Let's look at the 1 draw and the 1 blow on a C harmonica. The 1 draw is the note D and the 1 blow is the note C. When playing a 1 draw bend, you can bend down to whatever note is between these two notes. Looking at the chromatic scale above, that gives you the note D-flat. When playing a 2 draw bend, you can bend down to whatever is between the G of the 2 draw and E of the 2 blow. This gives you the notes G-flat and F. Follow this process up to the 6 draw.

At the seventh hole the harmonica does a back flip of sorts. On holes 1 through 6, the draw notes are higher than the blow notes (1 draw D is higher in the scale than 1 blow C for example). On the seventh through tenth holes the blows are now higher than the draws. This means that you'll bend the blow notes now. The same rule applies for the blow notes… whatever pitches are between the blow and draw reed are what you can bend.

Diagramed below are all the bends available on the C harmonica. Each slash (') represents a half step bend (3 = 3 draw, 3' = 3 draw half step bend, 3" = 3 draw whole step bend and 3''' = 3 draw minor third bend).

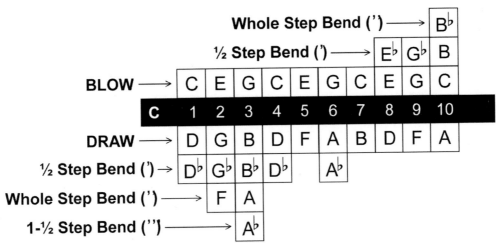

Bending Exercises

Your first goal is to bend as far as you can on each of the holes in Example 1.4. Most students find the 6, 5 and 4 draw the easiest holes to bend. Take note that the 5 draw will not give you a full degree of a bend, it will bend down what is called a Quartertone. In other words, you will only hear a slight bend on the 5 draw, and that is correct. The 3 and 2 draw will be very challenging. Expect these two holes to take months before they start to bend consistently. Give yourself a couple weeks to work on these bends before moving on.

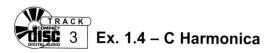

6   6'   6   5   5'   5   4   4'   4   3   3"   3   2   2"   2   1   1'   1

If you've spent a couple of weeks on Example 1.4 you can probably bend the 6, 5 and 4 decently, but find the 3 and 2 draw difficult to bend very far. If this is the case, focus on dropping your jaw slightly and humping the root of the tongue up more to access the back of your mouth better.

Even if your 3 and 2 draw are not consistently strong, let's still move on—they will get better with time. Most players find that their 3 draw jumps in pitch—from a slight bend to a full bend, with nothing in the middle. To remedy this, make sure that your tongue is following the curvature of the roof of your mouth. Chances are that you are moving the tongue back just fine, but the tongue isn't moving up high enough as you move your tongue back. A good visualization is to think like you have a marble sitting on top of your tongue. As you move your tongue back to bend, you must keep your tongue raised up to the roof of the mouth so that the marble doesn't fall down. This consistent distance to the roof of the mouth is what keeps the bend moving down in pitch smoothly until you achieve the deepest part of the bend. Resist the urge to tighten your mouth and ball up the tongue. Keep reminding yourself that you are simply tuning your mouth to the desired pitch to create a bend… no excessive force is needed for this.

Give yourself another couple of weeks to work on creating smooth bends, from unbent to a full bend with no jumps in pitch as you travel down. Don't forget to practice sliding out of the bend (from bent to unbent); in playing the harmonica we'll use both directions of the bend.

Stopping at the Bottom

The exercises below will help you to bend a note down and move to another note. Pay attention that your bend doesn't release slightly before going to the next note. Also pay attention that your next note isn't played flat because you haven't moved your tongue out of the bend embouchure quickly enough.

Ex. 1.5 – C Harmonica

6   6'   5   5'   4   4'   3   3"   2   2"   1   1'

Ex. 1.6 – C Harmonica

6 6' 5   5 5' 4   4 4' 3   3 3" 2   2 2" 1   1 1' 1+

After doing this on the C harmonica try these same exercises on the D, B-flat and A harmonicas. We don't just play one harmonica all the time; we play the harmonica that matches the key of song we're playing. The D is a higher-pitched harmonica; you will not need to move your tongue as far back to achieve the bends. The B-flat and A harmonicas are lower in pitch relative to the C harmonica and will require that you move your tongue further back to achieve each bend.

6

12 Bar Blues Bending Examples

Here are some 12 Bar Blues examples to work on the type of bending you've studied so far. All of the examples will continue to challenge your tongue blocking skills as well.

TRACK 4 — New Technique – Two Note Combinations

Note the addition of the 5 draw with the 4 draw in measure seven of Example 1.7. You can play this as just a 4 draw for a nice clean sound, or add the 5 draw for bluesy effect. As a rule of thumb, most blues players use a little bit of 5 draw with their 4 draw all the time. Be careful to not add too much 5 draw—it will sound overly dissonant. It's also common to add some 4 draw to the 3 draw. Any time you want a bigger sound for your 3 draw you can make this addition. Listen carefully to the recording to hear the different textures presented by how much of the upper note is allowed to sound.

TRACK 5 — TRACK 6 — Ex. 1.7 – C Harmonica (Play-Along Track is Track 6)

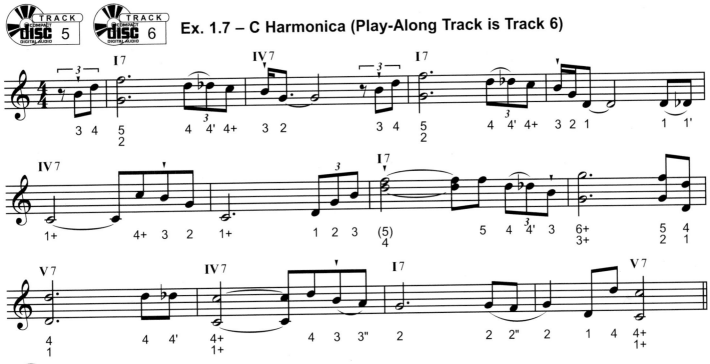

TRACK 7 — New Technique – Quartertone 3 Draw Bend

Another rule of thumb for blues harmonica is to play the 3 draw slightly bent most of the time (we're speaking of 2nd Position here). The bend is not as far as a half step bend—it's between the natural draw note and the half step bend, called the Quartertone. Listen carefully to the recording to match this pitch. One of the easiest ways to obtain the quartertone bend is to play a dip and not let the bend release to its natural pitch. Once you get used to the tongue positioning of this you can just bring the tongue to the proper place in the mouth and hit the 3 draw like this all the time. The only time this doesn't apply is when playing quickly past the 3, like in a triplet or sixteenth note run at a medium tempo; the listener can't tell the nuance in pitch at that speed. Example 1.8 will use the dip notation to indicate where the quartertone is used on the 3 draw. In later examples we'll use a 3 draw half step bend notation (3') with a plus above the note head (+) to indicate that the note is to sound one quartertone higher than what is notated below. The 3' notated in the tablature will clue you in that there's a bend and the plus marking above the note head will indicate to not bend it so far.

Note that the 3 draw in measure five of the second chorus is bent down to exactly a half step. This matches the chord better on the IV chord. If you play a 3 draw-centered lick as your main lick (like the one used in the second chorus), you will most commonly bend the 3 draw down another quartertone to achieve the half step bend to match the flat-7th of the IV chord better.

Note the use of 3 blow at the end of the IV chord (fourth beat of measure six). Using 3 blow in place of 2 draw will help you to exhale all of the air built up on the previous licks and prepare you for more draw notes to come. Allow air as possible to escape. Make sure to close your nose for the following draw note. This will take some practice, but is a highly effective technique to balance your breath.

This will be your first time using a bend in the middle of a shake. There's nothing special you have to do for this; start your shake and just focus on moving your tongue back for a bend, not stopping the headshake.

Ex. 1.8 – A Harmonica (Play-Along Track is Track 9)

More Bending Exercises – Articulate Bending

Let's now finish our bending study with the last area of focus, being able to start a bend at any pitch. Example 1.9 starts with an unbent note and has you bend as far as that hole will allow you to bend. Once you have reached the bottom of the bend, lock everything in your bending embouchure in place and stop your air so that the note stops sounding. After pausing for a moment, start your air again and hopefully you'll have the full bend sounding again. After confirming that the bend is sounding, release the note back up to its natural pitch. Don't worry if you can't play the deepest bend on the 3 and 2 draws… this will come with time and practice.

 Ex. 1.9 – C Harmonica

6 6' 6' 6 5 5' 5' 5 4 4' 4' 4 3 3''' 3''' 3 2 2" 2" 2 1 1' 1' 1

After you have practiced this exercise a number of times try to play the second half of each measure twice. We're trying to develop a muscle memory for where the tongue needs to be placed for each bend. This is demonstrated below for the 4 draw.

Ex. 1.10 – C Harmonica

4 4' 4' 4 4' 4

After a while of practicing this you should be ready to start notes in the bent position. Try the following example. Remember to give yourself enough time before each bend to place your tongue into position and confirm that it feels correct for the bend you're about to play. With daily repetitive practice you'll be able to lock in all of these bends.

Ex. 1.11 – C Harmonica

6' 6   5' 5   4' 4   3''' 3   2" 2   1' 1

Below is an excellent exercise to develop control of our most common bends (this was shown to me by instructor Gary Smith). Pay attention that your bends are strong and that you release quickly enough in order to not affect non-bent notes (commonly students have lazy tongue movement and the lower hole of the exercise gets bent unintentionally). Take note that we are not going to the full bend on the 3 draw. We will use the 3 draw whole step bend (3") from now on. The 3 draw whole step and a half bend (3''') is not commonly used in second position playing, and continuing to practice the fullest bend right now will only cause intonation trouble (playing notes out of tune).

Ex. 1.12 – C Harmonica

4' 4 5 4 4' 3   3" 3 4 3 3" 2   2" 2 3 2 2" 1

Play this exercise every time you pick up the harmonica. Strive for good pitch and a smooth rhythm.

Chromatic Scale

The 2 draw and 3 draw have more than one note available to them. So far we have just studied how to get to the bottom of a bend; we'll now work on every note available to us. Notated below are notes from holes 1 through 7 with every bend available. Work with the recording to make sure you're sounding each note with good intonation (a note that is intonated well is not slightly flat or slightly sharp—it's dead on pitch). When practicing this away from this recording make sure to use a piano or other pitch-generating device to make sure your bends are on pitch.

TRACK CD 11 Ex. 1.13 – C Harmonica

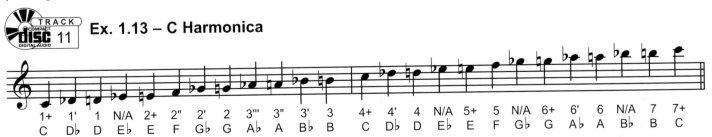

1+	1'	1	N/A	2+	2"	2'	2	3'''	3"	3'	3	4+	4'	4	N/A	5+	5	N/A	6+	6'	6	N/A	7	7+
C	Db	D	Eb	E	F	Gb	G	Ab	A	Bb	B	C	Db	D	Eb	E	F	Gb	G	Ab	A	Bb	B	C

9

Bending Example Song – "Feelin' Good"

"Feelin' Good" will really give you a bending workout. Some of the bends will be very challenging, though the slow tempo will make them accessible. Take your time and give yourself at least three months to work on this song. We'll use an "A" harmonica in this song.

First Chorus (Head)

Note the use of a lighter (unbent) 3 draw for the head. This gives room to build as the song goes on with a more bluesy presentation of the 3 draw. Pay attention that your 3 draw half step bend (3') is at proper pitch for the IV chord (see below). Also note that where pulls are notated, they are best played where the tongue just lifts off the face of the harmonica for a rounder, softer sound (we don't want the articulation of the pull for this song).

Ex. 1.14

Second Chorus

This is a slight variation of the head (reference the full transcription on page 14).

Third Chorus

Drop your jaw and tongue as well as opening your throat to play the 1 draw with as big a tone as possible. Play the chords at the end of measure two very softly.

Ex. 1.15

Fourth Chorus

Drop your jaw and open your throat to help the 2 draw whole step bend (2") sound with good tone. Raising your tongue from the root will give you a deeper bend than moving the middle of the tongue back. The bends used for the V-IV-I lick (measures nine and ten) will be very challenging—though worth the work. This type of lick is used by great players and arpeggiate the notes of the chord (plays the notes of the chord one after another). This type of bending is key to becoming an advanced player.

Ex. 1.16

Fifth Chorus

Note the use of the open and closed cup on the IV chord (measures five and six). For the closed cup simply play with your hands closed—cupping as much sound as possible in your hands for a muted sound. For the open cup simply play with your hands open—giving you a brighter sound. This works well for acoustic (playing in front of a vocal microphone) or amplified (cupping a bullet microphone through a tube amplifier—like that used for this recording).

Ex. 1.17

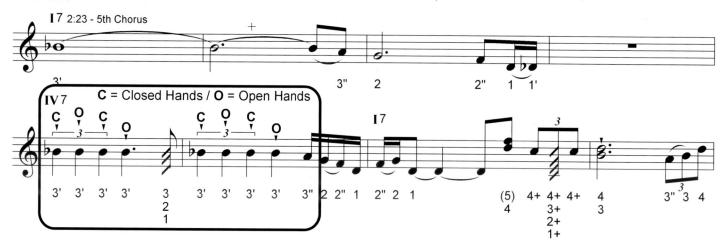

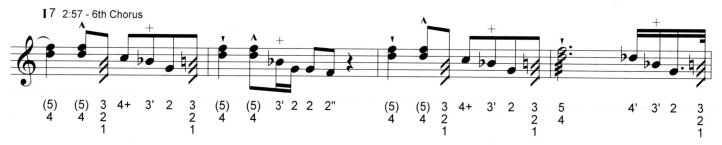

Sixth Chorus — TRACK disc 17

The second beat of the first measure brings a new technique called a Cut. A cut is the opposite of a dip. Start the note unbent and then bend it quickly for a sharply articulated lowering of pitch. This is notated with an upside down "v."

Ex. 1.18

Seventh & Eighth Chorus — TRACK disc 18 / TRACK disc 19

Keep your volume down to accompany John Garcia on guitar here. When playing amplified, cup up more to achieve a more bassy tone. If playing acoustically, close your cup more and play closer to the mic.

Ninth Chorus — TRACK disc 20

This is a nice relaxed chorus to help bring the head back.

Tenth Chorus — TRACK disc 21

The head returns to end the song. Watch your intonation (how well you play notes—in this case bends—in tune) on the last two notes.

Ex. 1.19

What To Say To The Band
- Key of E
- Medium-Slow Blues with a Delta Feel
- From the I (One Chord)
- Standard Ending

Feelin' Good

By David Barrett . A Harmonica in 2nd Position (Key of E)
Album: "Serious Fun" with John Garcia

Ex. 1.20

Chapter 2 – Advanced Tongue Blocking

You've already learned the main meat and potatoes of tongue blocking in book one—slaps, pulls and octaves. Most of your advanced study in tongue blocking will now be focused on articulation and mixture of application. With that said… here are some more advanced tongue blocking techniques to practice.

Five-Hole Octaves

All of the octaves you've studied so far have your lips placed over four holes, blocking two holes in the middle with your tongue. This four-hole embouchure works for all blow notes from the 4th hole and above. The draw is a different case.

The 1 draw (D on a C harmonica) and 4 draw (D) will give you octave D's. The 2 draw (G) and 5 draw (F) is not an octave, but the interval of a minor 7th; this gives you a dissonant sound (not an octave, but cool to use for bluesy effect). Looking above the 5 draw (F) you'll not find a G to match the 2 draw pitch. The 3 draw (B) and 6 draw (A) is not an octave, but again the interval of a minor 7th. Looking above the 6 draw you'll find a B to match the 3 draw pitch on the 7 draw. To obtain octaves from the 7th hole and above you'll need to use a five-hole octave embouchure—your lips over five holes and your tongue blocking the three in the middle.

To perform a five-hole octave you'll need to open your mouth wider (smiling and frowning at the same time will give you a very wide mouth). You might find it easier to cover five holes if you place a little bit more of the harmonica into your mouth. Try to hit any of the following octaves in the following exercise. You might find sliding to the right as you open your mouth makes finding the five-hole octave a little bit easier for now.

 Ex. 2.1 – C Harmonica

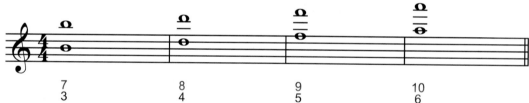

The challenge of playing five-hole octaves is when they are mixed with blow octaves, which are four-hole octaves. Try the exercise below.

Ex. 2.2 – C Harmonica

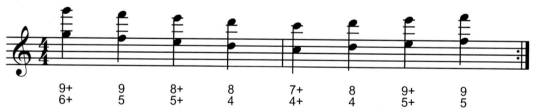

The key to performing octaves on the high end of the harmonica is to think about two things:

1) <u>Think wide for all draws and narrow for all blows</u>. Most players are not wide enough for the draws and are too wide for the blows (they're stuck in the middle). When playing, exaggerate how open you play for draws and exaggerate how small you close down for blows. Play Example 2.2 again with this in mind.

2) <u>When moving, move in half-hole increments</u>. When opening your mouth, both the left side and the right side of your mouth are moving—exactly a half of a hole in each direction. The same happens, but in the opposite direction, when you close down for the blow. As you go down in notes (first measure), move down a half of a hole for each note that you play. As you go up in

notes (second measure), move up a half of a hole for each note that you play. Play Example 2.2 again with this in mind.

Let's now play an exercise that uses both four-hole and five-hole octaves. Like all of the examples in this second book, it's power-packed full of technique—take your time and play it many times slowly before attempting to play along with the recorded example. You'll of course gain lick vocabulary from this piece, but our main focus is technique development, so that you can copy and use anything that you hear from great harmonica players. The chugging found between main licks can be left out at first (notes in parentheses) to make the example easier to play.

Ex. 2.3 – A Harmonica (Play-Along Track is Track 26)

The use of five-hole octaves in blues for the most part is a new technique (though it was used in pre-war [WW2] blues and country blues from the 1920's to the late 1940's). George "Harmonica" Smith became the primary force behind the use of the chromatic harmonica in the blues. The chromatic harmonica requires a five-hole embouchure to play octaves anywhere on the instrument. George Smith was also a killer diatonic harmonica player. It just makes sense that a player proficient on the chromatic harmonica would tend to use some of the larger embouchures, such as the five-hole octave on the diatonic harmonica—and he did. The two players that he deeply influenced, Rod Piazza and William Clarke, also became masters of the chromatic and diatonic harmonicas. Both Rod and Bill continued refining the role of the chromatic harmonica in the blues. A common technique to both players was (Bill is now unfortunately no longer with us) the use of octaves on the chromatic. In much of their soloing on the chromatic harmonica, the main lines—the most powerful lines—were played in octaves. Just like George Smith, they both transferred this technique to the diatonic harmonica in a much larger way than any other player before them.

When you listen to Bill Clarke or Rod Piazza you'll hear a snap to their octaves—specifically their draw octaves. When you play Example 2.3 you'll probably notice a softness, or lack of snap to your octave notes. To achieve this articulation we'll need to dig into the **Side-Pull** and **Pull-Slap**.

Side Pull

The side pull is performed by blocking all five holes in your embouchure with your tongue (just like a pull). This is generally achieved by sticking your tongue out more. If this doesn't work, then you're using too much of the tip of your tongue—tilt the face of the harmonica down a bit, place more harmonica in your mouth and use more of the top of the tongue deeper in the mouth. This will give you access to the wider part of the tongue, making it easier to cover five holes. Once you have covered all five holes, draw your tongue back, leaving the tip-top of the tongue still on the harmonica so that the octave sounds. Try this on the following example. Use a slight cough for all blow octaves.

Ex. 2.4 – C Harmonica

The side pull is used on draw octaves (or any draw note played in a tongue block when you're not looking for a slap sound) when you need some articulation, but don't need to really accent the note(s). When you want to accent the notes strongly, that's where the pull-slap comes in.

 **Octave Pull-Slap**

The pull-slap starts with a pull and is then immediately followed by a slap into an octave. The movement is very fast. The listener should hear one composite sound. Try Example 2.4 again, but with the octave pull-slap for the draws instead of the side-pull.

Octave Pull-Slap with Upbeat Pulls

The pull-slap really shines when used in conjunction with upbeat pulls. When performing a pull on the upbeat and a slap on the downbeat, the pull and slap share the same chord—there's no separation. By using pull-slaps on the downbeat you'll now achieve a very articulate line. Again, this is a draw-only technique. Try the example below with all of the downbeat octaves as octave pull-slaps.

Ex. 2.5 – C Harmonica

In Example 2.6 below I've taken Example 2.3 and added articulation markings for you. "C" is a blow cough. "PS" is an octave pull-slap.

Ex. 2.6 – A Harmonica

Pull-Slap Single Notes

Pull-slaps are not only used in octaves—they're used anywhere you want a little snap to your tongue block slaps. To perform the pull-slap on a single note, start with a pull and quickly follow it with a slap. Again, this technique creates one composite sound—don't let the pull and slap sound like two different functions. The exercise below is similar to Example 2.5 except for the use of blow notes. When the blow notes are used, use coughs instead of pull-slaps. It's a general rule in the post war Chicago blues style of harmonica playing to not articulate your blow notes except for a cough—draw notes can use any variety of articulations.

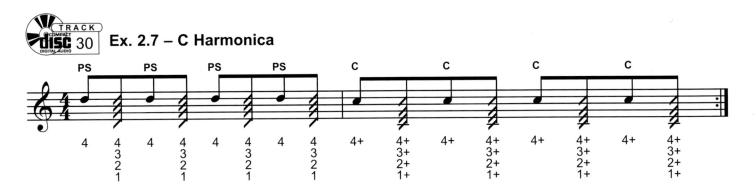

Ex. 2.7 – C Harmonica

Sometimes blow pull-slaps can be used when you're specifically looking for a "spity" sound. Demonstrated below is a lick similar to what Sonny Boy Williamson II (Rice Miller) would play using pull-slaps on both the draw and blow notes.

Ex. 2.8 – C Harmonica

Where would you use pull-slaps—octaves or single? Whenever you want notes to be more distinct. When a classic blues harmonica player plays, pull-slaps are a regular part of the articulation vocabulary. (Many times, experienced players use this articulation and are unaware of the mechanics that are making it happen. You purchased this book to speed up your progress—this is why we're speaking of this now and not waiting for your body to hopefully stumble across it in the future).

Chapter 3 – Final Example Songs

Our final two examples songs will provide more context to the techniques you've been studying. "Feeling Good" challenged you for many months to develop good bending skills. The following two songs will help to implement bending with a lot more tongue blocking technique. These are very challenging songs (especially "Lick Train"), so take your time and don't get down on yourself for not developing as fast you think you should. Give yourself a year to be able to perform the main three study songs presented in this book with the provided Play-Along Tracks. Your final exam is to play the tunes with your band or a local jam session. There's nothing better than working hard to learn a tune and getting the chance to perform it live… a true reward for the hours of dedicated practice!

"Serious Fun"

The slower tempo of "Serious Fun" makes it our best song to study first. We'll use an "A" harmonica again in the key of "E."

TRACK disc 31 First Chorus (Head)

The licks played are fairly simple, but presented with a big tone. The main focus here is to achieve the "big" sound of playing two note combinations (dirty notes). Experiment with how much 5 draw you add to your 4 draw. Notice that when adding just a touch of the 5 draw it has a thickening effect, but when adding more 5 draw, it starts to overpower the 4 draw. Practice playing through your bullet mic and amplifier to work on how much 5 draw is needed to add the color you hear on the recording. Note that the guitar plays in unison the entire head; this is common to add weight to the most important part of the song—the head.

Ex. 3.1

TRACK disc 32 Second Chorus (Head Two)

Sometimes there are two main themes in a song. For this song, head two is the main theme that returns between the soloists—head one only returns at the last chorus.

TRACK disc 33 Third Chorus

Note the continued use of two-note textures for our main lick. Note the lower bends to match the IV Chord.

Ex. 3.2

Fourth Chorus

The opening lick needs no articulation—resist the urge to use any. Measure seven brings our first use of 5-hole octaves. Take your time and focus on achieving a good, clean octave after each upbeat pull. In measures nine and ten, triplet quarter notes are used. Triplet quarter notes give the feel of a floating rhythm; listen carefully to the recording to make sure you stay in time here. Triplet quarter notes offer a wonderful rhythmic change that's used often by good players.

Ex. 3.3

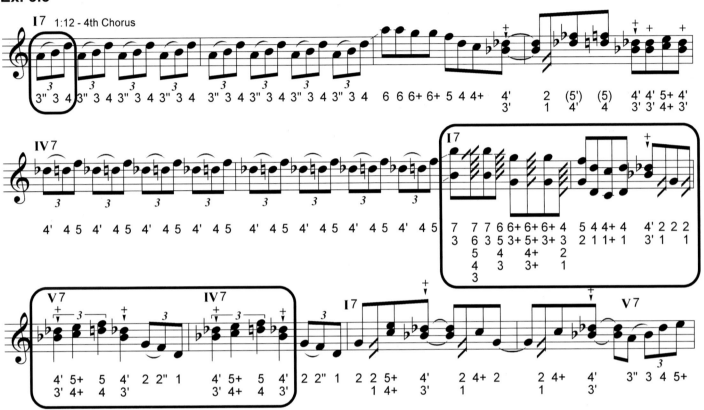

Fifth Chorus

This is the chorus where you kick into overdrive with thicker, heavier textures and generally louder playing. Note the interesting lick in measure seven. I picked up the basic form of this lick from Paul deLay. Though it's a C Major Arpeggio (the notes of the C Major Chord played one after another), which matches the IV chord, this lick works well over any chord.

The lick starting at measure nine is one of my favorite licks that traverse the entire range of the harmonica. This is a lick I picked up from William Clarke. The sixteenth note pulls and octaves that immediately follow the pulls will be challenging for you to play in time. As always, slow down your practice tempo to really work on these challenging licks. Focus on tilting the face of the harmonica down slightly and placing the harmonica a little deeper in your mouth. This will access the wider part of the tongue, making it easier to cover five holes with your tongue on the high-end draw pulls and pull-slap octaves. Pull-slaps are recommended for all of the draw octaves to help them to "pop." Lack of articulation in a passage like this will make it sound lethargic and lack power.

It's hard to find material that utilizes the high-end of the harmonica. Any licks that traverse higher than the 6 blow are worth spending some time learning. Another tool you can use to become more proficient at the high-end is to transfer licks that are played on the 2 draw to the 6 blow and move them up one octave to the 6 blow to 9 blow. Stay away from licks that use bending, since they won't transfer over. Taking licks from a range that you're comfortable with and moving them up is a great way to give you familiarity with the high-end.

Ex. 3.4

![TRACK 36] **Sixth Chorus**

The sixth chorus of the solo is the bridge. A Bridge brings together two elements in a song. In this case, the bridge signals the repeat of the second head, and after the second head a new soloist. A bridge deviates from the form—changing the order the chords are played, adding new chords or changing the overall length of the form. A bridge could use a couple of these elements, or all of them.... it just depends on the song. In this case, the ii chord is the new chord. The form changes from a 12 Bar form to an 8 Bar form. The chords last for one measure each and are as follows: IV-I-IV-I-IV-I-ii-V. This is a very common bridge form. Notice how this section of the song gives a much-needed break from the standard 12 Bar Blues form.

![TRACK 37] **Seventh Chorus**

The seventh chorus brings the repeat of head two. After head two the guitarist solos. Note that when I start my solo that it starts on the V chord (measure nine) of the second head. This is a nice way to introduce the new soloist a bit earlier than the standard beginning of the form. The guitarist (John Garcia) will do the same for his solo. You'll see this noted below, before measure nine.

Ex. 3.5

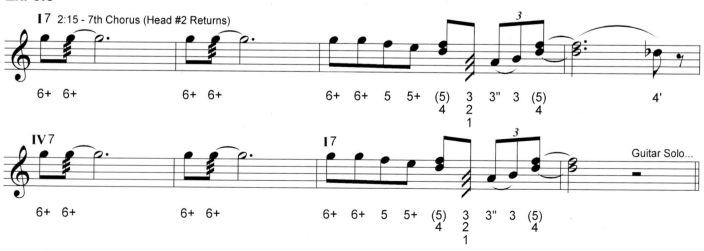

Serious Fun

Album: "Serious Fun" with John Garcia
By David Barrett . A Harmonica in 2nd Position (Key of E)

Ex. 3.6

What To Say To The Band
- Key of E
- Shuffle
- From the I (One Chord)
- Watch me for the bridge after each solo (In other words, you'll signal them when the bridge is coming)
- It's an 8-bar bridge with the chords: IV-I-IV-I-IV-I-ii-V

The only tricky thing in this song is the bridge. Luckily this is a very common bridge chord progression, so you shouldn't get any weird looks from the band. If you have a moment to spend with the guitarist, play for him or her both heads and ask them to play in unison with you. This adds weight to the two main themes of the song.

"Lick Train"

"Lick Train" is your graduation song! The amount of technique, how they're mixed and the tempo of this song will keep you busy for a long time. Again, all of these main study songs are very challenging. I'm a believer in giving students graduated study songs, but I'm also a believer in challenging them with songs that are a little above their skill level. Why? With dedicated practice you'll develop your skills much faster. So, dig in and enjoy the process! Again we'll use an "A" harmonica.

First Chorus (Head)

40 This is the busiest head I've every written… there's a lot going on. The main lick is based on the rhythm created by the downbeat slap and upbeat pull. The opening is very reminiscent of "Walter's Boogie," by Big Walter Horton. Note the slight 5 draw added to the pulls and single notes to dirty-up the 4 draw. Try the opening line without the addition of the 5 draw at first to get a feel for the line, then add the 5 draw and be careful not to add too much (it can overpower the line). Watch your rhythm on the triplet quarter notes in measure four. This is where the band will come in, so don't throw their sense of your timing off by being off on the rhythm here (practicing with a metronome can be very helpful). Notice that I start the song alone, with the band coming in on the IV chord. This is a great way to focus the attention immediately on the harmonica. The jump from 6 blow to the lower bend notes on the IV chord will take some time. The turnaround will also take some time, to control the bends well on the A harmonica.

Ex. 3.7

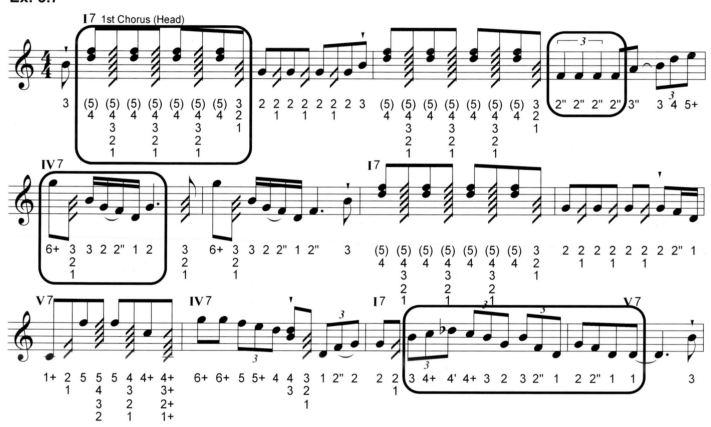

Second Chorus (Head w/Variation)

This is a repeat of the head with a variation on measure four.

Third Chorus

The head uses a lot of range of the harmonica; it makes sense to go lower on the harp for the first solo chorus.

Fourth Chorus

In the fourth chorus the band breaks on the I chord. The harp plays the same rhythm as the head, helping to unify the song. Note the addition again of the upper note to thicken the passage. The 7 draw flutter on the IV chord is not common. The 7 draw doesn't match the IV chord notes very well (the B clashes with the B-flat of the chord). Remember, bluesy means dissonance—the more dissonance, the more bluesy it sounds. So, what can be considered a wrong note is a right note when played with conviction and followed up well. Notice the strong buildup to the fifth chorus with the triplet passage.

Ex. 3.8

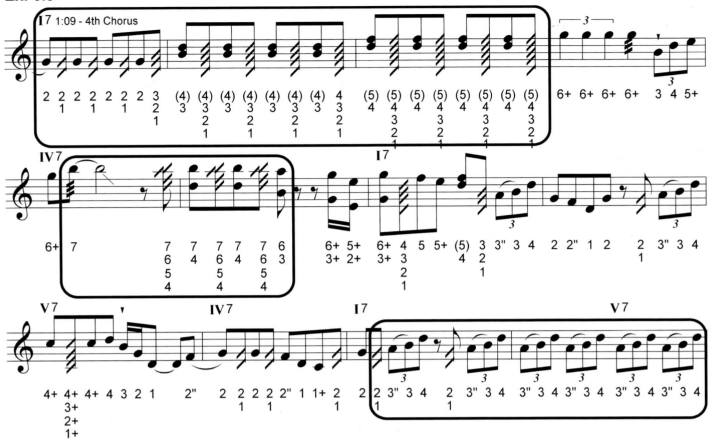

Fifth Chorus

This is the chorus where you kick into overdrive with thicker, heavier textures and general louder playing. Notice the extensive use of two-note combinations to dirty up the sound in the opening lick. The addition of the 6 draw to the 5 draw is not as commonplace in second position, but works really nicely here. Measures three and four continue the thick presentation with octaves, fake octaves (like the 2 draw/5 draw), pulls and shakes. Take your time to develop the correct combination of upper notes in this passage. Accuracy in this passage and the next is very important—otherwise, it will sound sloppy.

Ex. 3.9

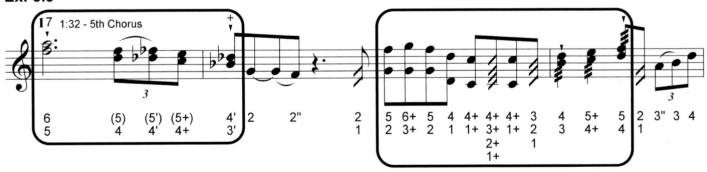

Sixth Chorus

In the sixth chorus the band breaks on the I again. The harp plays the same line as chorus four, up one octave. This is a great way to incorporate some high-end playing.

29

Ex. 3.10

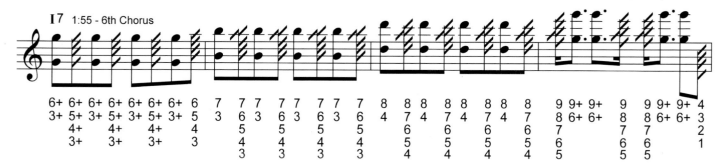

disc 46 TRACK
Seventh Chorus (Head Returns)

The head returns to finish the song in the last chorus. Note the nice walkup in octaves to a variation on the IV chord. This gives a nice climax to the song without deviating too far from the main theme of the head. The blow bend on the 10 blow can be overpowering if you play directly on mic. Make a point to open your hands a bit when playing high blow bends to save the audience from a shockingly high and loud passage.

Ex. 3.11

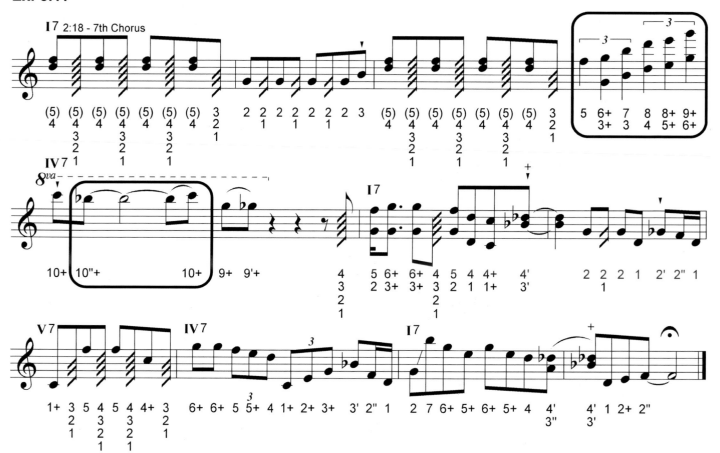

What To Say To The Band
- Key of E
- Shuffle
- I'll take the I (one chord), meet me on the IV. Watch me for similar breaks throughout the song.

Lick Train

Album: "Serious Fun" with John Garcia
By David Barrett . A Harmonica in 2nd Position (Key of E)

NOTES

NOTES